Indian Beadwork

INDIAN

GRAY-WOLF.

BEADWORK

WRITTEN AND
ILLUSTRATED BY

ROBERT HOFSINDE
(Gray-Wolf)

WILLIAM MORROW & CO., Inc. New York, 1958

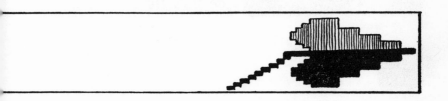

8   9   10   75

Library of Congress Catalog Card No. 58-5251

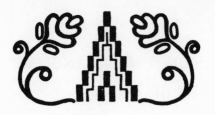

To Reyna Jean

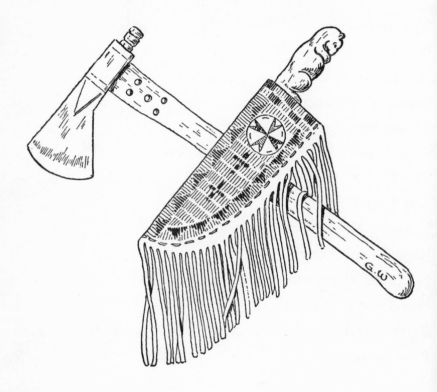

Contents

GRAY·WOLF·

Introduction

Indian beadwork tells a story. The type of beadwork shows us what tribe it came from and when
it was produced. The color and design reveal, in
many cases, the story of the Indian who once
owned and wore the beaded item. Moccasins and
medicine bags often speak the loudest, especially
when the moccasins are made for ceremonial
purposes.

The history of this beadwork began with the
Indian's use of paint. Indians used colored earth,
clays, and rocks, as well as plants and bark, to
make their dyes. All these were dried, pounded,
and ground into a fine powder, which was then
mixed with water or animal fat to make paint.
The paint was rubbed into their garments, which
were made of animal skins, or used for decoration
on their faces and bodies. Sometimes the paints

were boiled in water and then used for staining robes, willow back rests, or basket materials.

Then one day an Indian woman dropped a few porcupine quills into the boiling colored water, and the quills became tinted with the soft shades. The woman tried making ornaments with these quills. Possibly her first attempt was a quilled band, which she might have used to trim a new pair of moccasins for her husband. The experiment was successful, and the discovery spread among many other Indian groups. In some such way quill embroidery slowly developed into a fine art. This art is found only among our American Indians.

When the white man came from across the Big Waters, he brought many new things with him. Some were bad things, but among the good things were Italian colored beads. At first there were only a few of these beads, but the Indians began to discover that they could use them for embroidery in place of quills. The beads proved to be a good trade item between white men and Indians, so more and more were imported. Early records show that the Mohawks had beads as early as

1616. By 1711 the Woodland Indians in the Great Lakes region, the Ojibwa, Menominee, and Winnebago, were using them. From 1780 through the early 1800's, beads spread from New York to the Rockies. Still, quillwork held sway over bead embroidery as late as 1830.

The early beads, which were rather large, were known as pony beads. They were used from 1800 through 1840. Then a very small bead, called a seed bead, became popular. They were used on garments made during the period between 1840 and 1870. Finally a larger seed bead was introduced, and it is still used today. The diagram at the right shows the comparative sizes of these beads in the order of their appearance.

At first, when beads were still not plentiful and Indians were reluctant to change the old ways completely, quills and beads were often used together in the same piece of embroidery. Old war shirts have broad bands of quillwork edged in beads. Moccasins were also decorated this way. Soon, however, the quills were put aside, and beads replaced them entirely. Fully beaded vests,

11

blanket strips, breechcloths, leggings, and moccasins were very common when the warriors gathered for council meetings.

The Woodland people used floral designs in their embroidery and worked on crude looms, and the Plains Indians worked with geometric designs. Crow and Blackfeet Indians, however, combined both types of design in their work.

The plainsmen, scouts, and Mountain Men soon realized the value of buckskin clothes. They wore better than their rough, homespun cloth, and many of these early adventurers adopted bead decorations along with their fringed buckskin jackets. They also used beaded knife sheaths, belt bags, and moccasins when they could get them.

Different tribes used different methods of working with beads, such as loom work, lazy stitch, overlay beading, and straight-line beading. All these methods are described in this book, although the articles to be made are planned for modern use. A specific design is suggested for each article, but each design can easily be adapted for use on many other items.

GRAY·WOLF·

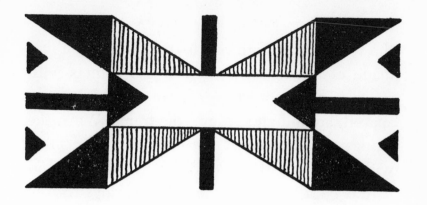

1

The Bead Loom

THE Ojibwa Indians have practiced the art of bead weaving for many years. At one time they used a crude type of bow loom, which had a strip of birch bark tied at each end separating the loom strings. This loom was later replaced by the frame loom. It was simpler and easier to handle, and wider strips of beadwork could be woven on it.

The picture of the Ojibwa woman shows how this loom was usually worked. The loom rested against a stake driven into the ground, so that the weaver had both hands free. The frame was made of ash and was tied at the corners with sinew. The loom strings were wound, evenly spaced, around and around the frame. When the strings on the front of the loom had been filled with the design, the beadwork was pulled around to the back, bringing the empty strings on the back to the front.

An adaptation of this loom, suitable for our purposes, is shown in Figure A. The materials needed to make it are:

One piece of white pine, 6 inches by 30 inches by ½ inch thick.

Two pieces of white pine, 4 inches by 6 inches by ½ inch thick.

Ten small screws, about 1 inch long.

One curtain spring, about ⅜ inch in diameter. May be bought in five-and-ten-cent store or hardware shop.

Two small, large-headed carpet tacks.

Fasten the two 4-by-6-inch pieces in an upright position to the ends of the 6-by-30-inch piece. The

long side of the small piece is placed against the end of the large piece. Each end piece is held in place with three screws, as shown in B. Now cut the curtain spring into two lengths, each about 7½ inches long. With a pair of pliers, pull each end of the coil out, as in C.

Fasten a screw to each outer edge of the upright ends and wrap a pulled strand from the spring around one of them. Then stretch the spring across the top edge of the upright, pulling the coils slightly apart to relieve the tension. Now coil the other loose end of the spring around the screw on the other outer edge of the upright. Then tighten the screws, and they will hold the wire in place, as shown in D.

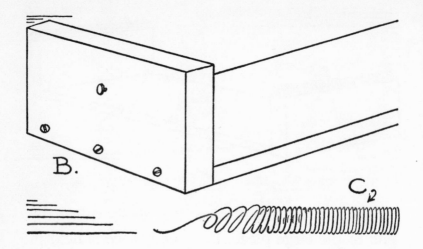

B.

C₂

When both uprights have been fitted with springs, hammer a small tack into the center of the outer end of each upright, as indicated with the black dot in D.

The loom is now ready for stringing. Number 8 cotton or linen thread should be used. Knot one end of the thread to the tack in the center of one of the uprights. Pass it up to the spring and between two coils. Bring the thread in a straight line across the length of the loom, through the two opposite coils in the other spring, and around the tack in the second end piece. Then bring the

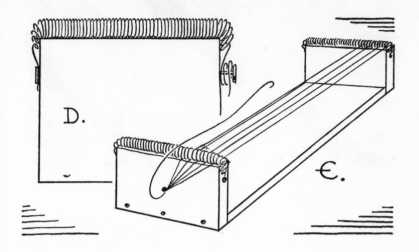

thread back again in the same way. Continue this stringing, as in E., until the required number of strands are in place.

For a strip of beadwork 19 beads wide, 20 loom strings are needed. The number of strings is always one more than the number of beads in the width of the design. Since most beadwork has a center line, the width of the work is usually an odd number of beads.

When you string the loom, make the strands as tight as you can without breaking them. This makes the work easier.

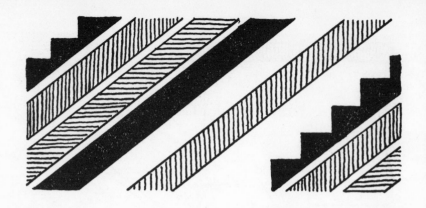

2

Beaded Belts

BEADED belts are attractive with slacks or summer dresses. Select the size and design you like best. The design in A. is 15 beads wide; the one in B. is 23. The color chart shows suggested colors, but you can change the colors to suit your own needs. Be sure, however, that the outlines of the design are done in a color that will contrast with the background. Black or dark blue is good on a light blue background, and white or yellow will stand out well against red.

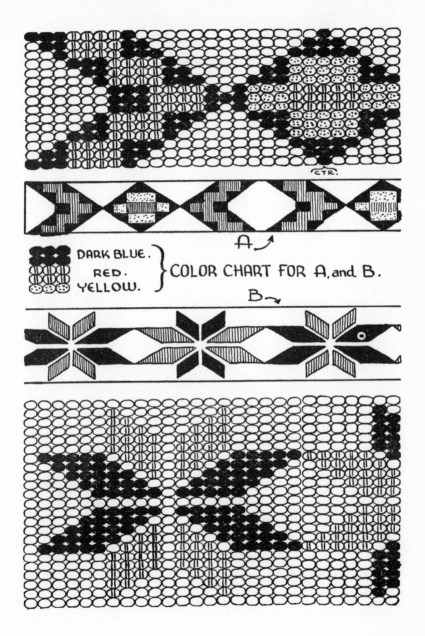

CTR.

A ↗

DARK BLUE.
RED.
YELLOW.
} COLOR CHART FOR A, and B.

B ↘

Materials for the beadwork throughout this book are as follows:

Beads of various colors, either in vials or hanks.

Thread, No. 40.

One package of fine bead needles.

A piece of beeswax, or a candle stub, for waxing the thread.

Graph paper, for drawing designs.

Colored crayons.

You will also need a little patience. Even an experienced beadworker will, from time to time, have a little trouble getting the first row of beads on the loom. From then on, however, the beading usually goes smoothly.

Thread a needle with a fairly long thread. Double it and knot the ends. Then wax it. This thread is then tied to the outer loom string nearest you at the left end, as in C.

Use a small shallow dish to hold the beads. Sea shells are good and so are small party ash

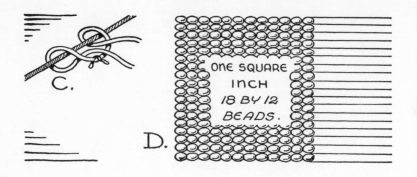

C.

D. ONE SQUARE INCH 18 BY 12 BEADS.

trays. Pour a *few* beads of each color into the dish. Do not pour *all* the beads in at once, for you may upset the container and it is a nuisance hunting for a great many spilled beads. The following number of beads are needed for one square inch of loom work: 18 beads across the loom strings, 12 beads along the loom strings. See D.

Pick up the beads needed for the first row of the pattern, following the indicated color changes, with the point of the bead needle. This is faster than picking up each bead in your fingers. Slide the beads down the thread to the loom strings. Then pass the needle *under* the loom strings. With your left index finger move the beads into position between the strings; one bead goes between

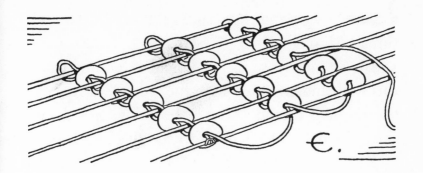

each pair of strings. When all the beads are in place, pass the needle back through the beads again. This time, however, the needle must pass *over* the loom strings, as indicated in E.

When the needle is through all the beads for the second time, pull the thread so that the beads fit tightly together. Then repeat this weaving row by row, pulling each row tight and pushing it close to the preceding one.

If a bead breaks, as it sometimes does, or if the needle must be removed from the work for any other reason, *pull it out backwards by the thread.* Never try to get it out point first.

When it is time to change to a new thread, avoid knotting the new thread to the old. Start the new weaving by passing the needle and thread through 5 or 6 beads of the last row. Leave an inch or so of the thread extending from this row, and continue with the work as if it were the original thread. After a few rows are done, this thread is cut off close to the beadwork.

To end a thread without knotting, pass the needle once around the outer loom string and then through 4 or 5 beads of the next-to-last row. Now the thread can be cut.

When the bead strip is completed, but still on the loom, the ends must be finished off. Place a piece of gummed paper tape below the loom strings, as in F. Then fold the ends back over the loom strings. The strings will be glued in place. Cut through the loom strings along the outer edge of this tape.

The beadwork is now free and ready to be sewed to a foundation. A good leather belt makes a sturdy base, or a good cloth or patent-leather belt may be used.

Place the bead strip on the face of the belt, one end near the buckle, the other near the last hole,

28

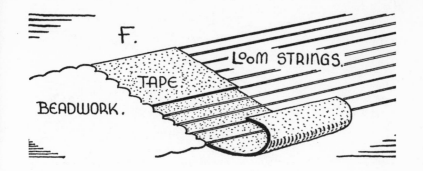

F.

LOOM STRINGS.

TAPE

BEADWORK.

as in G. Sew the beadwork to the belt with a regular needle and waxed thread, as shown in H. Knot the thread and start sewing from the inside of the foundation. The needle should come through at the corner of the first bead in the first row and on the inner side of the outer loom string. Loop the needle and thread over this loom string,

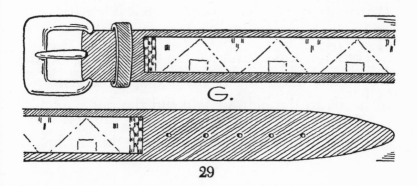

G.

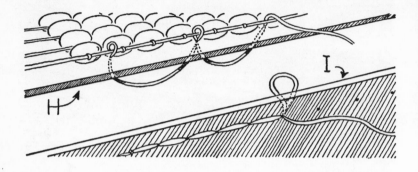

and pass the needle down again through the *same*
hole it came up in. Skip 2 or 3 beads along the
edge, and repeat the sewing. The under view of
the stitching appears in I.

Work along one side for 7 or 8 inches; then sew
a similar distance along the other edge. Continue
working both sides in this way. You will discover
that the beadwork does *not* lie flat on the belt.
It will hump a little. When the belt is worn, however, the humps will straighten out.

Fold the tape strips at the ends of the beadwork back under the beads and sew the last row
of beads to the belt, as you did the outer edges.

3

Beaded Necklaces

NECKLACES, of one type or another, were worn by both men and women in many Indian tribes. Some were purely ornamental; others were medicine charms. Some carried a special meaning. The necklaces made from the claws of eagles or bears, for example, showed that the wearer was a mighty hunter.

The type described here is of the ornamental variety. The design, shown in A., has an open space running through most of the center. This space runs through the middle of the loom strands. In each row there are 7 beads on each side of the center division. Allowing for the extra string needed to make the center space, string the loom with 16 strands. To hold the two parts of the necklace together, weave one section without a center space. There will then be 15 beads in each row here. The beginning and end of this section are indicated by the arrows 1 and 2 in B.

Start the beadwork at arrow 1 and work up to arrow 2. Allow 6 inches between the end of the loom and the beginning of this strip. When this section is completed, work each half of the necklace separately, first one, then the other, up to the far end of the loom. To work the section below the diamond, turn the loom around and weave from the end of the diamond to the end of the loom, one half at a time. The design in this section ends in two points, as shown in B.

To make these points, add 5 rows of white beads, 7 beads on each side of the center space, after you complete the last triangular shape. Then sew in only 5 beads on each side, then 3,

3. 4. 5. 6.

←C.

D.

←A.

DK. BLUE.

LT. BLUE.

WHITE.

RED.

2→

B.
→

1→

THIS IS THE
UPPER HALF
OF DIAMOND
1-2 IN 'B'.

G.
W.

and finally 1. Make sure that these beads are centered, as shown in C. Gather the free, outer loom string with the thread when you sew the short rows, and keep the extra strings tight.

When you finish the two points, cut the loom strings as close to the spring as possible. There will be 8 strings extending from each point. Gather them together and pass them through a large tube bead, as in D. Push the tube bead up to the single bead at the end point, and string from 10 to 12 regular beads on each pair of strings, making 4 end strings. Tie the last of these beads on each string in place with a square knot. This will make the bead hang vertically, and it will hold the other beads in place. See details in D. These bead tassels will form the pendant of the necklace.

To complete the necklace at the other end of the loom, cut the loom strings close to the spring. Because of the open space in the middle of the design, there will be two separate straight endings here. See lines 3-4, 5-6 in A. To join endings 3-4 and 5-6, gather the threads from each of them

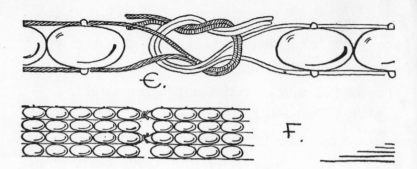

E.

F.

in pairs, as in E. Knot them together in square knots, and the finished joint will appear as in F.

The necklace in G. is made much like the one described above. In this one, however, the solid section is sewed at one end of the necklace. Another difference is that it ends in a beaded fringe, and you will have to allow space on the loom strings for it. Do this by starting the work away from the end of the loom.

Still a third necklace design is shown in H. It has been drawn so that you may use it for a necklace in the style of A. or G. If you plan to follow style G. (the necklace with the fringed end), start the work at the arrow above the two end points.

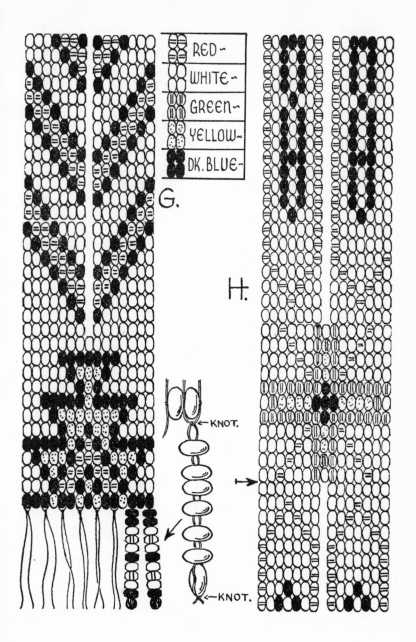

RED –
WHITE –
GREEN –
YELLOW –
DK. BLUE –

G.

H.

← KNOT.

← KNOT.

4

Beaded Headbands

INDIAN headbands were made and used to keep the hair in place and out of the eyes. The Indian warrior also used them to hold his feather ornaments, or his large coup feather, in their proper position.

Many girls today find them attractive and helpful, and they are not very difficult to make. The common metal hair clamp looks particularly nice when it is covered with a strip of beadwork, as

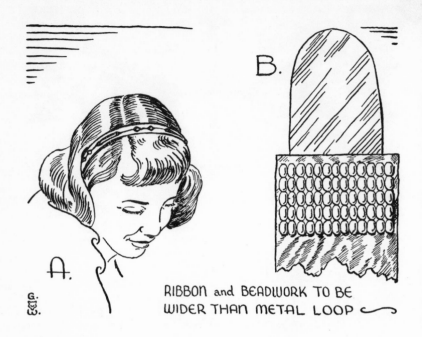

RIBBON and BEADWORK TO BE
WIDER THAN METAL LOOP

shown in A. Buy the clamp first in a drug, depart-
ment, or five-and-ten-cent store; then make the
bead strip to fit it. Decide on the proper size by
stringing a few beads on a thread. Place the thread
across the band or clamp. If one bead extends on
each side, as in B., that number of beads is the
correct width. Now string the loom with the number of strings needed for rows of this size.

When you draw the design for the beadwork,

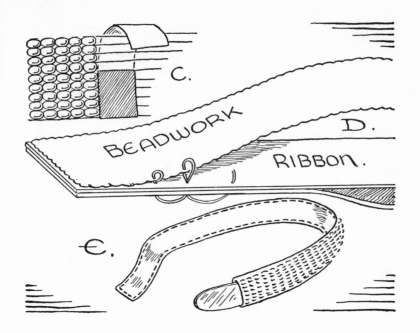

C.

BEADWORK

D.

RIBBON.

E.

make sure it is the exact length of the clamp.
When you complete the actual beadwork, end it
by the taping method in C., covering the loom
strings at both ends with gummed paper.

Cut the beadwork from the loom and sew it
with very tiny stitches to a good grade of ribbon
exactly the same width as the bead strip. See D.
Sew up one end and the sides, as shown, but leave
the other end open to the last. The bead strip and

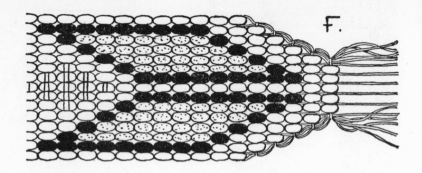

F.

the ribbon now form a long, narrow tube. Carefully slide the metal clamp into this tube, as in E. When the clamp is covered, sew up the open end.

A design for a tie-on type of headband is shown in F. This headband is wider and needs no backing of any kind. It is 15 beads wide, so 16 loom strings are needed. The tapered ends are made in much the same manner as those described in the Necklace chapter.

Various widths and designs to be used are shown in diagrams G., H., and I.

In making these headbands, work the broader section on the loom first, leaving enough room to add the tapered ends later. Remember it is better to make the band a little too short than too long.

42

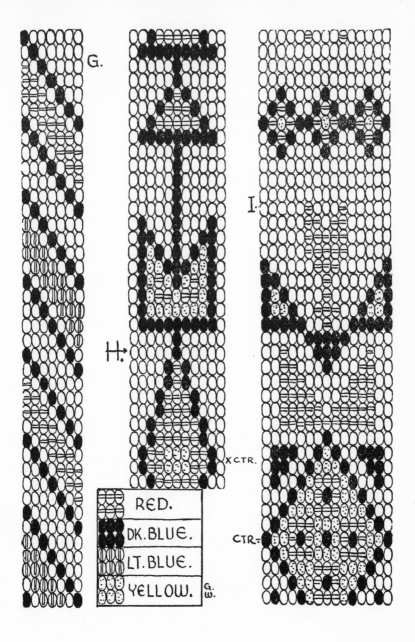

G.

I.

H.

X CTR.

CTR.

RED.

DK. BLUE.

LT. BLUE.

YELLOW.

G.
W.

The completed work for this type of headband is *not* taped but is cut from the loom on the outside of the upright ends.

Gather together all the loom strings and tie them in a single knot, as in J. These ends are then divided into three parts and braided. Tie another knot at the final end, as in K.

Place the band over your hair and tie the braided ends in a small bow under the hair in back.

Designs in several other chapters are suitable for this work, although you will have to add the end design in F. to them. If you use a design with a center motif and different figures on either side of it, start the beadwork in the middle of the loom and work out from the center design, one side at a time.

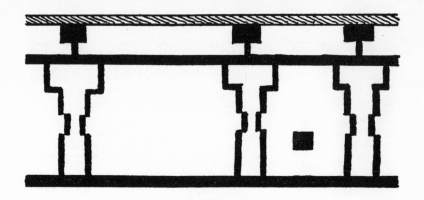

5

Beaded Bracelets

THIS beadwork is very easy, for a small bracelet can be made in about one hour. You may want one to match your necklace, and it also makes a nice gift.

On the loom described earlier it is possible to make three bracelets at once, even allowing for sufficient space between the bead strips and the ends. The beadwork is finished by the taping method. See A.

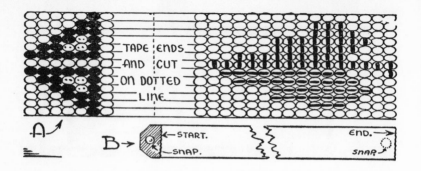

Select a section from the necklace design for one bracelet design. The other two designs may be taken from those shown in this chapter. The length of the bead strip will, of course, depend upon the measurement of your wrist or of the person's for whom it will be made. The beadwork should be just long enough so that the two ends of the bracelet will come together evenly when it is worn.

A soft strip of leather or a good grade of ribbon is needed for the foundation. This foundation strip should be a little wider than the bead strip and long enough to overlap itself by ¾ of an inch. At one end of it, sew one half of a small snap, as in B. At the other end on the reverse side, sew the

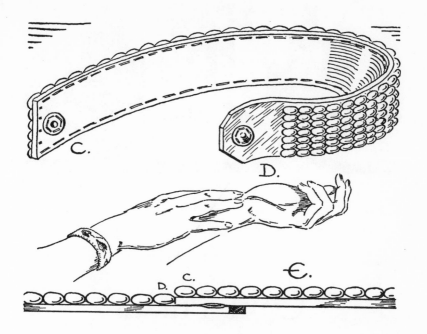

other half. Then sew the beadwork to the foundation, as in B. Different views of the snaps are
shown in C. and D.

The beadwork will cover the stitching on the
reverse side of this last snap, and the overlap will
cover both snaps when they are fastened together.
When the bracelet is worn, the overlap and the
bead ends will appear as they do in E.

6

Coin Purses

Trinket bags and small medicine bags were used a great deal in the Indians' everyday life. One reason was that Indian clothing had no pockets. Even though both girls and boys have pockets to use today, pocketbooks, school bags, and coin purses are still very useful.

Two pieces of material are needed to make a coin purse, as shown in A. One piece forms the back of the purse and the front flap, and the other

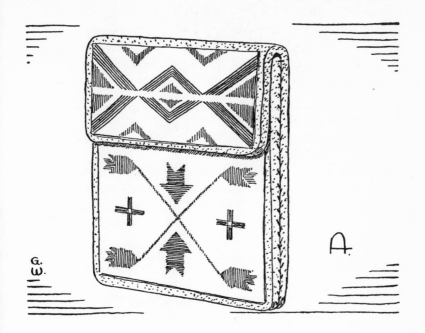

the front of the purse. The purse pattern is drawn
in B. Use the full drawing for the pattern of the
back and the flap. The pattern for the front starts
at the bottom and ends at the dotted line marked
fold. Draw the full pattern on a piece of paper,
using the measurements indicated. Cut it out
along the outer edges; then trace it very carefully
onto a soft piece of leather or heavy felt.

The bead design in C. is for the flap. It includes

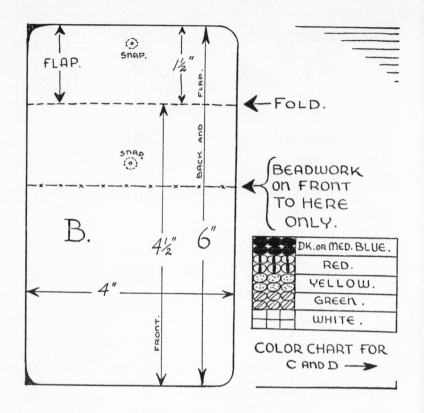

FLAP.

SNAP.

1½"

FLAP.

←FOLD.

SNAP.

BACK AND

BEADWORK
ON FRONT
TO HERE
ONLY.

B.

4½"   6"

← 4" →

FRONT.

	DK. OR MED. BLUE.
	RED.
	YELLOW.
	GREEN.
	WHITE.

COLOR CHART FOR
C AND D ——→

the left half and a small section of the right half.
The exact center line is indicated. To complete
the right half, follow the design of the left half
in reverse.

The design for the front section, shown in D.,
is drawn and should be followed in the same way.

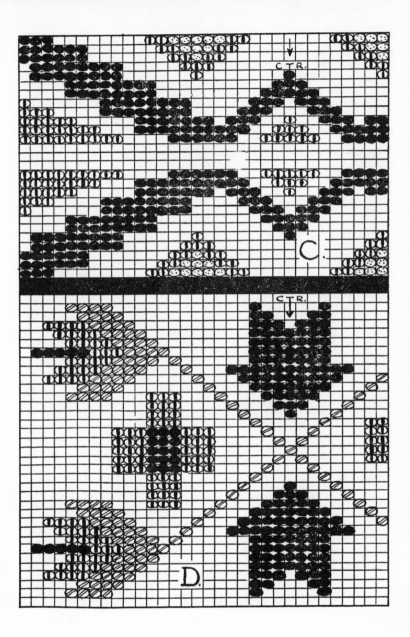

C.

CTR.

CTR.

D.

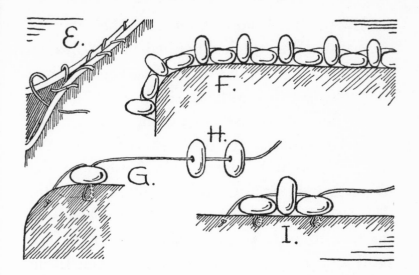

The beadwork on this piece does *not* extend all the way to the top of the pattern, shown in B.

The ends of these two pieces of beadwork are finished with the taping method, as is the case with all beadwork which will be sewn to a foundation.

Before you sew the bead strip to the flap, sew half a snap fastener to the underside of the flap, a little below center. Then sew the other half of the snap to the front piece of the bag above the beadwork. The location of both snap halves is shown in B. and marked *snap*.

Now sew the beadwork pieces to their foundations, using the stitch described in the Beaded Belts chapter. Finally sew the front and back of the purse together with the stitch shown in E.

The decorative bead edging, shown in F., is an attractive variation for this coin purse. Much of the old Indian beadwork was finished in this manner. Start, as in G., by sewing 1 bead to the edge of the foundation. Next string 2 beads on the thread, as in H. Slide them against the first bead and sew the second one down, as in I. The middle bead will stand on edge. Repeat this procedure, 2 beads at a time, until the entire edge is decorated. It will look like the drawing F. Use any one of the colors in the beadwork edge, but it is better not to use the color of the background. The edge should contrast with the beadwork as much as possible.

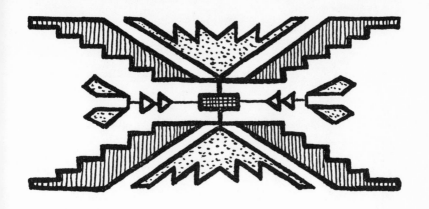

7

The Lazy Stitch

THIS chapter describes an entirely different method of beading. Since the beads will now be sewed directly on the foundation material, the loom is not needed. The sewing is done with a stitch commonly called the *lazy stitch*. It is found in nearly all the beadwork of the western Plains Indians.

The beads are sewed in rows of 8 in separate bands on the foundation material. The bands of

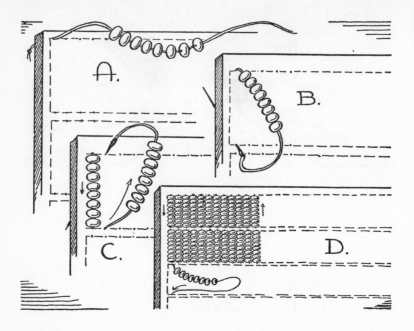

beads are 8 beads wide. One square inch of this work is formed by 2 bands of 12 rows each. See D. The number of beads needed to make a square inch in the lazy stitch is less than in loom work, because of the needed space between the bands of beads.

As shown in A., pass a double thread through the foundation from beneath, starting at the upper left-hand corner. String 8 beads on the thread and pass the needle through the material at the lower

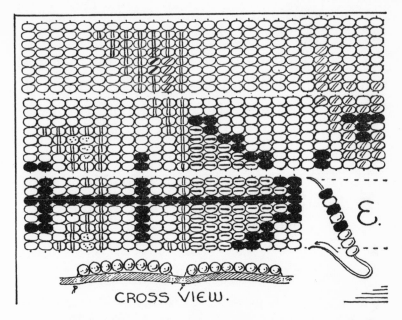

CROSS VIEW.

left-hand corner, directly below the top of the
row, as in B. Bring the needle out again next to
the last hole, as in C. Now string 8 more beads
on the thread and insert the needle into the material next to the first hole, making sure that the
two rows fit tightly together. Start the third row
like the first. The sewing continues in this fash-
ion, up and down, until the end of the foundation band is reached. Follow the various colors
indicated in the design when selecting the beads

59

for each row, and the same pattern will form in the beadwork.

Do not pull the beads too tight, for then the material will buckle under the beads. Although this type of beading is not as smooth and even as that made on the loom, this beadwork is very attractive when done carefully.

The first row of beads on the second band must start directly in line with the first row on the first band. If it does not, the design will be crooked. See D.

On each band there will be narrow spaces between the rows, as in E. This means that the finished work will have a ridgelike appearance. Be sure, however, that the spaces are no wider than is necessary.

It is wise to start with a small item when first trying the lazy-stitch method. This second type of coin purse described here will be just right.

Following drawings F. and G., outline your pattern on a piece of paper. Draw on it the bead design you will use from one of the suggestions given here. Now trace the design on the founda-

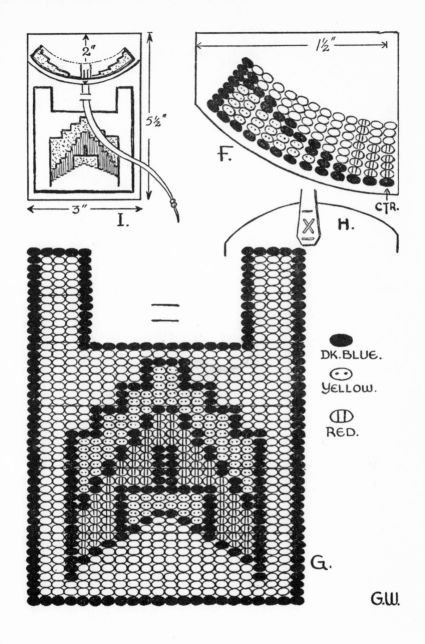

2"

5½"

3"

I.

1½"

F.

CTR.

H.

DK. BLUE.

YELLOW.

RED.

G.

G.W.

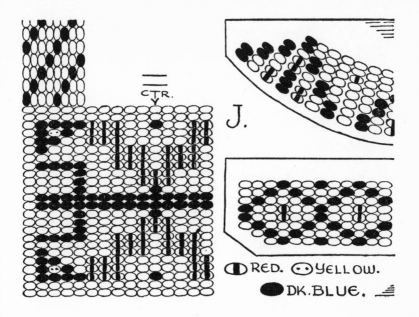

CTR.

J.

● RED. ☺ YELLOW. ● DK. BLUE.

tion material. This material may be either leather or felt.

This purse has a rounded, only partly beaded flap, instead of the straight flap on the first coin purse. The beadwork on the front stops at the lower edge of the flap, but two straight bands of beadwork continue up each side, as in G.

When the beading is completed, sew the two halves of the purse together as you did on the other purse. In place of the closing snap, sew a thin leather thong to the underside of the flap, as in H. Just above the beadwork on the front piece, cut two small slits, like those shown in G. Then pass the thong through them, as in I.

String one large tube bead to the end of the thong and hold it in place with a knot. When the purse is opened, the thong will not pull out. To close the purse, just pull the end of the thong.

Designs for another front piece and two more flaps are drawn in J.

GRAY·WOLF.

8
Belt Bags

MOST Indian men and women usually hung a decorated buckskin bag from their belts. Some Indians carried personal trinkets in them, but the warriors put their medicine charms in them.

This belt bag still has many uses today. It makes an extra, handy pocket during summer-camp days, when one is dressed in a T shirt and shorts. It is especially useful for carrying things on camping trips or over water.

The belt bag is longer than the coin purse, and it ends in a decorative fringe. A loop is made on the back, so it can be fastened to a belt.

Make a paper pattern by following the measurements in A. and B. There are three parts to it—front piece, back piece, and strip for the belt loop.

In the beadwork patterns F. and G., the flap is designed with a curve. It can also be rectangular, as in H. The beads are usually sewed with the lazy stitch. If the flap is straight, however, the beadwork for it and the front can be made on the loom and sewed on the foundation later.

After the beading is done and *before* the two halves are stitched together, the loop should be sewed on the back. Sew the top end of the loop, the end nearest the flap fold, first, as in C. Then fold the loop over and down, and attach the lower end, as in D.

The bottom edges of the front and back pieces, above the fringe, are sewed together with the overhand stitch, shown in E. Do *not* cut the fringe until the bag is finished. If the fringes are cut

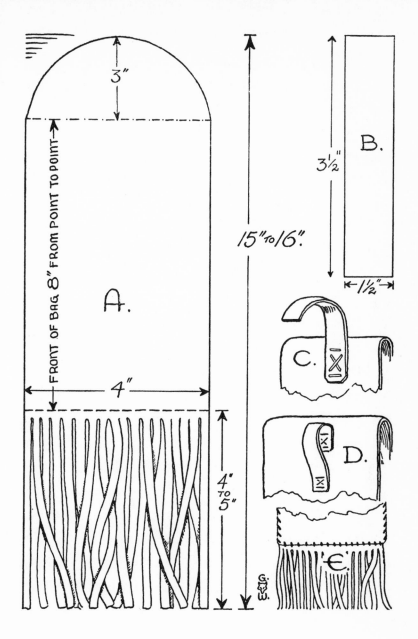

3"

FRONT OF BAG 8" FROM POINT TO POINT

A.

4"

4" TO 5"

15" TO 16".

B.

3½"

1½"

C.

D.

E.

G. W.

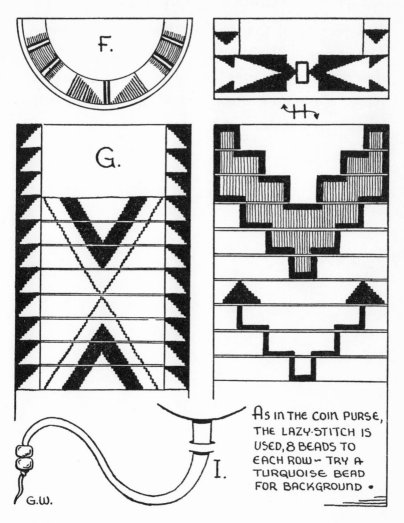

F.

G.

As in the coin purse, the lazy-stitch is used, 8 beads to each row — try a turquoise bead for background.

I.

G.W.

before the bag is sewed together, they will get tangled in the thread.

A picture of the tie-string fastener is shown in I. It is made like the tie string on the coin purse described in Chapter 7. You may use a snap fastener or even a button instead, but the tie string is what the Indians used.

9

Beaded Knife Sheaths

AN attractive beaded covering can be made for the sheath of a scout or hunting knife. Both Indians and Mountain Men used such decorated sheaths. This chapter will describe how to make a Plains type and a Woodland type.

To make a pattern for the covering of a Plains sheath, use a large piece of paper with a dotted line marked down the center of it. Place the long straight edge of the sheath along the dotted line,

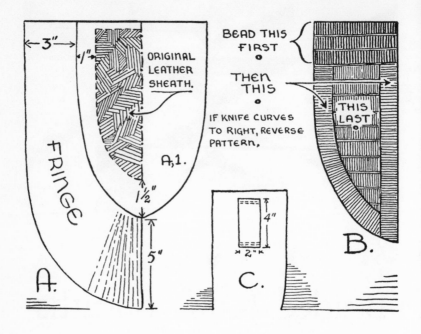

and draw an outline of the sheath. This is the shaded area shown in A. To the left of the curved edge of this outline, measure 1 inch at the top; then measure 1½ inches straight down from the point at the bottom. Connect these points with a curved line paralleling the original outline. To the left of this new line measure 3 inches at the top; then measure 5 inches from the point at the bottom. These two points are also connected with

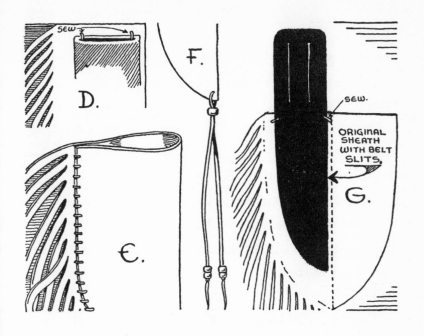

a curved line. This second area is for the fringe. See A.

Fold the pattern along the dotted line and trace the outline of the second curve, but do not trace the fringe curve. Then open up the paper again, and cut out the full pattern. Trace this pattern onto a piece of soft leather or chamois, and trim it carefully along the edges.

The design for the sheath is shown in H. Draw

it on a piece of paper. Then fold your cut-out leather piece in half, and trace the design upon the unfringed section. See B.

Start the beading by filling in several rows straight across the top. Then do the designs along the edges, and finally fill in the center. These steps are also indicated in B.

When the beadwork is finished, make a belt loop from a piece of leather 2 inches wide by 4 inches long. This loop should be sewed onto the back of the fringed half close to the top, as shown in C.

Remove the loop from the original sheath, and make a hole in each of the top corners of the sheath. Attach it to the fringed half of the new sheath by sewing through the holes with a strong thread, as in D. Fold the beaded section over to cover the original sheath, and sew together the curved edges of the new sheath along the line shown in E. Then, with a pair of sharp scissors, cut a very fine fringe along the curved edge of the sheath.

If you prefer a sheath without a fringe, elimi-

COLOR SUGGESTIONS.

WHITE BACKGROUND:
- DK. BLUE.
- LT. BLUE.
- RED.

RED BACKGROUND:
- BLACK.
- GREEN.
- LT. BLUE.

LT. BLUE BACKGROUND:
- DK. BLUE.
- RED.
- YELLOW.

○ BACKGROUND
   BEADS IN "H".

IF THE KNIFE SHEATH IS
WIDER THAN THE 16 BEADS
SHOWN HERE, WIDEN TOP
BAND AND CENTER "STEPS"
AS BELOW.

G.W.

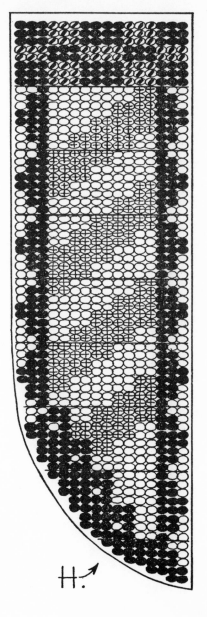

H.

nate it from your pattern at the beginning. You can add decoration to this sheath by making holes at the front and the back of the bottom point and pulling a thong through them. Knot the thong, and add a few large tube beads to the ends. See F.

Some sheaths have an extra piece of leather which extends beyond the top. This piece has two vertical slits in it, so that a belt can pass through them. If your sheath is of this type, there is no need to make the belt loop. Just sew the original sheath to the new one as described, and let the slitted part extend above, as shown in G.

Some hunting knives have double-edged blades; for a knife of this kind, the Woodland sheath mentioned earlier is just right. Here again we need a pattern. See J. Draw the outline of this sheath in the center of a piece of paper. At the top measure out ½ of an inch from the curved edge on the left. Do the same on the right. See J., 1 and 2. Then measure 1 inch down from the bottom point. Connect 1 and 2 with the bottom point by drawing a curved line paralleling the original sheath. Then draw a 2-inch line straight up from 1; do the same at 2. Now connect the top points of these lines (3 and 4) with two arcs. See J. This extended section will contain the belt slits.

Cut out this pattern and trace another outline of it. Do not draw the belt-slit section on the second pattern. See K. Use these patterns to draw and cut out two leather pieces.

Draw the Woodland design, shown in L., and trace it onto the smaller piece of leather which will be the front of your sheath. To make this design, we shall employ a third beading method, one that was often used by the Blackfeet and the Crow Indians. The Woodland Indians used it in some of their work, especially for filling in the background of a floral design. In its finished state, it looks a good deal like loom work; but because it is sewed directly to the material and is fastened down all across each row, it is sturdier than loom work and thus better suited for articles that are handled often.

After the design is traced upon the front of the

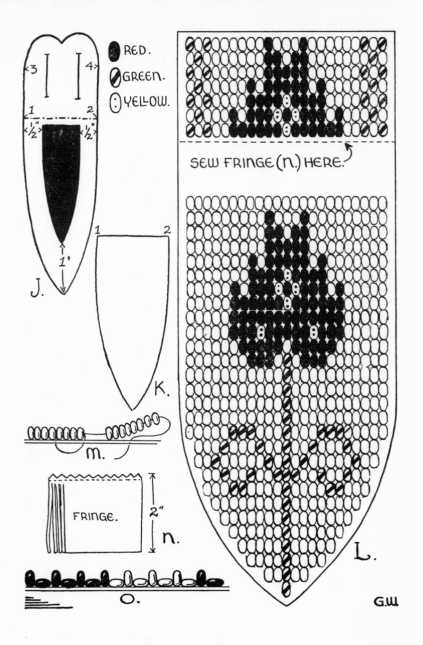

RED.

GREEN.

YELLOW.

SEW FRINGE (n.) HERE.

J.

K.

m.

FRINGE.

2"

n.

O.

L.

G.W.

sheath, start beading in horizontal rows. String from 6 to 8 beads on your thread, as in M., and sew them down. Your needle and thread are now underneath the leather piece. Bring them to the top again by pulling the needle through the leather into the center of the line of beads just sewed down. Then bring the needle and thread out through the last beads, and string another 8 onto the thread. These are again sewed down, and the above process is repeated. Since each new group of beads will be attached to the last half of the previous group, the beads will fit as closely together as if they were all strung on one continuous thread.

As you work along, change to the various colors needed to form the design.

You will notice that there is an undecorated section near the top of design L. When the bead-work is completed, a 2-inch strip of leather, pinked at the top, is sewed to this space and cut into a very fine fringe, as shown in N.

To add a finishing touch, the edges of the sheath should now be beaded. Take two of the main colors used in your design and alternate them; that is, sew on 7 dark blue beads, then 7 light blue ones. Also alternate the way in which you sew them on; that is, sew the first bead horizontally, the second standing on edge, and repeat. See O. Also bead the curved top of the back piece of the sheath—the belt-slit section. For further details on bead edgings, see the end of Chapter 6, "Coin Purses."

Make two vertical slits in the belt-slit section, so that your belt can pass through them. Now sew together the front and back pieces of the sheath.

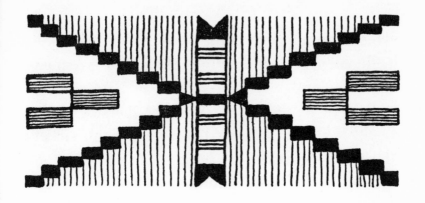

10

Beaded Book Covers

A BEADED book cover will protect your favorite book and make it more attractive. For such a cover, use soft calfskin, which can be bought in a hobby shop or a leather-supply store. One of the following colors is suggested: natural, red, dark green, or dark blue. Calfskin is commercially tanned and is therefore smooth on one side and rough or suèdelike on the other. It is best to do the beadwork on the suède side, as it creates a more rugged and appropriate effect. Beadwork

85

which has a background of white or light blue will look very well on any of the four above-mentioned colors.

Pattern A. should be cut to fit the size of the book. If you still have the original book jacket, it will be a good guide. Note that a strip ⅜ of an inch wide must be added to the top and the bottom of the cover, to allow for sewing down the edges.

Bead only the front of the cover. See B. for a suggested design. In this design the frame is 8 beads wide and sewed with the lazy stitch. The border of the center circle is also 8 beads wide. After you have finished the frame and the border, fill in the center design. Alternative designs for the frame and the center are shown in C.

When the beading is completed, fold the flaps inward and sew them at the top and the bottom with the squaw stitch, as shown in D. Continue this stitching across the middle section between the two flaps on the top and bottom edges. To insert the book into this beaded covering, fold back the hard cover, as shown in E. When the

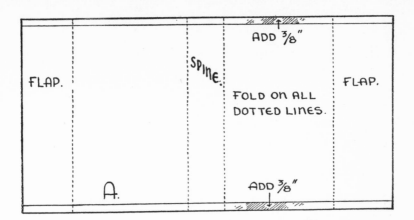

FLAP.

SPINE.

ADD ⅜"

FOLD ON ALL
DOTTED LINES.

FLAP.

A.

ADD ⅜"

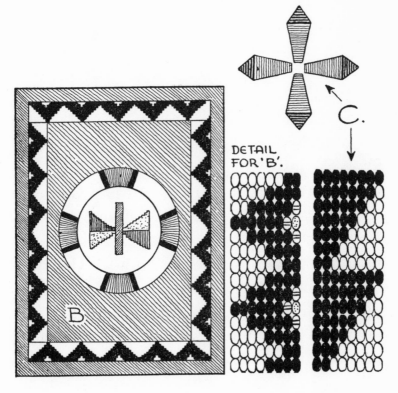

B.

C.

DETAIL
FOR 'B'.

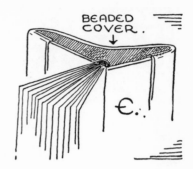

book is closed, the leather cover will fit smoothly over it.

You may also decorate your book cover with a strip of loom work. A design suggestion for this is shown in F. Cut the leather cover for your book. To determine the proper length of the bead strip, measure the width of your cover from the front edge to the far edge of the spine. After you have completed your loom work, finish off the ends with paper tape and sew the strip to the cover, slightly above the center, as in G. Both of these procedures are described in Chapter 2, "Beaded Belts."

If you sew the cover together by the method described earlier, you may want to add a bead

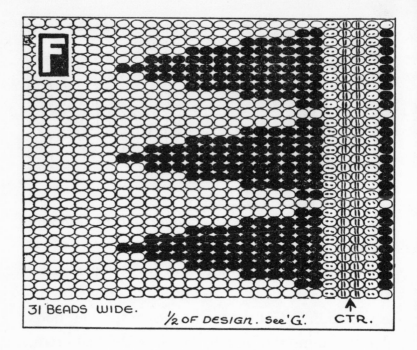

31 BEADS WIDE. ½ OF DESIGN. See 'G'. CTR.

edging to make it even more attractive. See the chapter on Coin Purses for a description of this edging.

Instead of this method of sewing the cover together, you can use a leather lacing around all of the edges, as shown in H. Punch holes evenly along the edges with a leather punch, and wind your lacing in and out of the holes. If this method

90

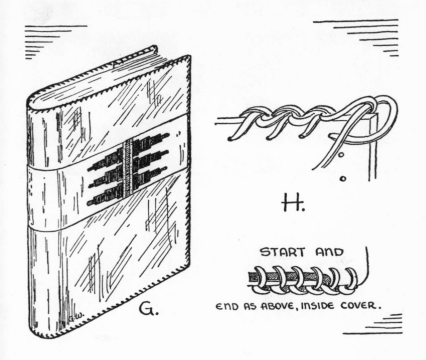

H.

START AND

END AS ABOVE, INSIDE COVER.

G.

is used, it is best to cut the flaps from the cover along the dotted lines instead of folding them. Then lace the flaps to the front and back covers of the book. The usual name for this lacing is gimp, and it sells for about three cents a yard in craft-supply stores.

Other cover designs are shown in the back of the book.

11

Northern Plains Moccasins

MOCCASINS are very comfortable for both indoor and outdoor wear. The Plains Indians made and wore two types of moccasins. One had a hard rawhide sole, and the other was a one-piece northern Plains moccasin. The following directions are for the latter type.

For indoor wear, a thick felt can be used to make these moccasins. However, you will need a sturdier material if you want to wear them outdoors; split cowhide is by far the best for this purpose. The pattern for the right foot is shown in A. By reversing this pattern after it has been drawn and cut out, you will have the pattern for the left foot.

Take a large piece of paper and place your shoeless foot upon it. Then, holding your pencil straight up and down, trace the outline of your foot. See the shaded area in A. Now make the following measurements on the pattern, using A.

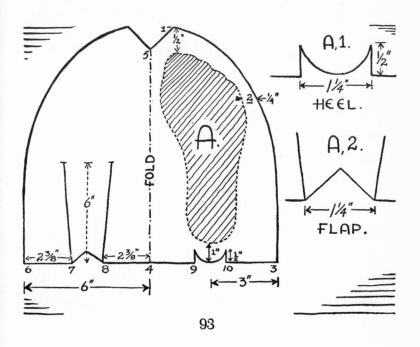

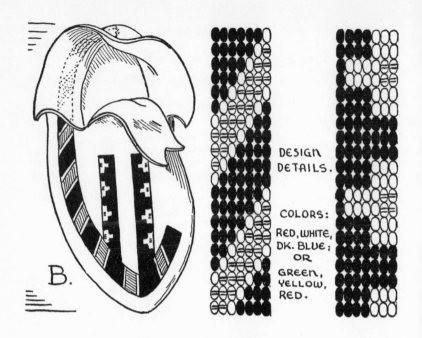

DESIGN
DETAILS.

COLORS:

RED, WHITE,
DK. BLUE;
OR
GREEN,
YELLOW,
RED.

B.

as your guide. Measure about ½ of an inch up from the tip of the big toe. This is point 1 in the diagram. Then, slanting your ruler downward from this point, draw a line 1½ inches long. The lower end of this line is point 5. Next measure ¼ of an inch to the right of the little toe. This is point 2. Then measure 1 inch straight down from the center of the heel. At the end of this 1-inch line, measure 3 inches out to the right. This is point 3.

94

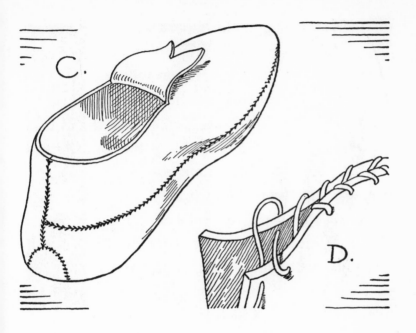

With a curved line, connect points 1, 2, and 3. To the left of the center heel line, measure out another 3 inches. This will give you point 4. Connect this in a straight dotted line with point 5. You will now have the sole of the moccasin pattern.

Cut along the outline from point 3, through points 2 and 1, to point 5; but do *not* cut along the dotted line. After this is done, fold the paper over along this center line, and draw a duplicate of the outline upon the other half of the paper. This will be the top section of your moccasin. Open the paper again, and you will have the entire pattern, except for the heel and tongue.

Next measure ½ of an inch below the center of the heel. To the left of this point measure out ⅝ of an inch. Do the same to the right. Then, from each of these points, draw a line ½ of an inch long. Now draw an arc connecting the top points of these lines. The lowest point of the arc will be midway between points 9 and 10. See A. and A.1. Cut out this heel piece, following the shape made by the two ½-inch lines and the arc.

On the top section draw two slightly tapered lines, about 6 inches deep, for the flap or tongue. The width of the top edge (see A., points 7 and 8) should be 1¼ inches. Also see A.2. Notice that a triangular piece is cut out of the flap on the top. Mark that on your pattern. Now cut out the flap, but do *not* cut too deeply at first. After you have tried the pattern on your foot, you may find that it fits too snugly over your instep. If that is the case, you can then make the slits longer.

When you have made certain that the paper pattern fits your foot, open it and place it flat upon the material you have chosen for your moccasins. Carefully outline this pattern on the material with a soft pencil. Remember to *reverse* the pattern for your left foot.

To decorate the moccasins, add bands of beads to the top section. This beadwork must be applied *before* the moccasins are stitched together. Since the tongue will cover part of the moccasin when it is folded over the top, plan your beadwork so that it will not be hidden by the tongue. See B. for a picture of the completed beadwork and for design details. The narrow designs shown in the chapter on Necklaces can also be used for beading moccasins.

When your beading is finished, bring together the edges of the moccasin, making sure they are even with each other. Sew up the edges with the squaw stitch, first along the long side seam. Now, to form the back seam, bring lines 6 to 7 and 8 to 4 together in a vertical position and sew them. See A. To finish the back seam, sew lines 4 to 9

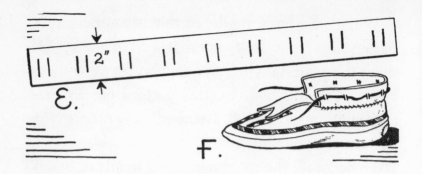

E.

F.

and 10 to 3 together in the same way. The small, rounded heel piece is then folded up and stitched into place, and the moccasin will appear as in C. See D. for the squaw stitch.

Now a cuff should be added to the moccasin. This consists of a strip of the same material from which the moccasin is made. It should be 2 inches wide and long enough to fit around the opening of the moccasin, from one side of the flap to the other. See E. Cut several pairs of slits in this cuff, as in E., and sew it to the top of the moccasin with the squaw stitch. A narrow tie string can now be passed through these slits and tied at the front of your foot. It will hold the moccasin securely in place. See F.

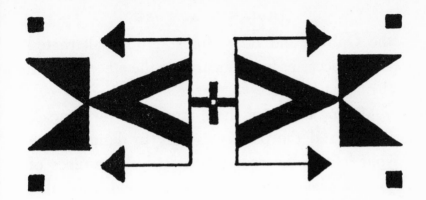

12

Woodland Moccasins

THIS chapter will describe how to make the type of moccasin worn by the Woodland Indians. Like the northern Plains moccasin described in the preceding chapter, this moccasin has a soft sole. The Indians living in the great forests of the North preferred this moccasin to the hard-soled type, because the pine needles on the ground made hard-soled moccasins slippery.

In this type of moccasin there is no difference between the left foot and the right foot. In fact, the Ojibwa and other forest groups alternated their moccasins from one foot to the other to make them last longer.

Making a pair of these moccasins for yourself is fun, and the pattern is easy to design. Place your foot in the center of a fairly large piece of paper. Then, with your pencil held vertically, trace the outline of your foot. As in A., measure 2 inches up from the tip of the big toe. Then find the broadest part of the foot on the right side, and from that point measure out 2 inches. Do the same on the left side. Now connect these three points with a curved line, as shown in A., and continue down each side in a straight line to a point 1 inch below the heel of the shaded outline. Connect these two bottom points with a straight line.

The instep piece, B., has the same shape as the large pattern, but is only one half its length. To obtain the width of the piece, loop a string around your foot at the base of your big toe. The width of the instep piece will be one third this measurement.

After the paper patterns for the moccasin and

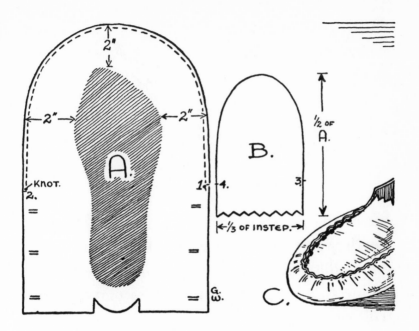

the instep piece have been fitted properly to your foot, trace them upon a good grade of split cowhide and cut the shapes out carefully. With a pair of pinking shears, cut along the top edge of the instep piece, as shown in B.

Next, pucker the moccasin by running a darning needle and a strong thread, doubled and waxed, along the curved edge of the large pattern from 1 to 2. See the dotted line in A. Sew in and

103

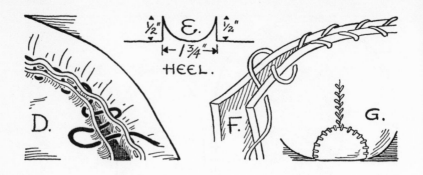

HEEL.

out of the material with short stitches of equal length. Then put the leather piece on the floor, stand on it, and slowly pull the end of the thread. As the thread is pulled, the entire curved piece will pucker up around your foot.

Attach the instep piece to the moccasin by bringing together 1 and 3, and 2 and 4, and sewing all the edges, except the pinked edge, to the puckered section. The finished instep piece will look like C. The method for sewing the instep piece to the moccasin is pictured in D.

When this work is finished on both moccasins, the straight back is folded up, and the edges are placed together. If the moccasin is too long, trim it to the proper length, and then cut the heel

notch. This should be 1¾ inches wide and ½ of an inch deep. See preceding chapter for details; also see E. Sew up the back seam, as in F.; then sew up the heel piece, as in G.

Cut three pairs of slits along each side of the moccasin, on the unpuckered part. See A. Draw a tie string through these slits. Now take another piece of cowhide and make a cuff 2½ inches deep and long enough to fit around the top of the moccasin. Make the lower edge slightly longer than the top. See H. Trim as shown, making the lower ends curved, and make a notch at the center of the lower edge. Sew the cuff to the top of the moccasin, using the squaw stitch, as shown in F. This cuff will cover the tie string. See I.

To decorate the moccasins, use a new beading method—the overlay stitch. Leaves, flowers, and tendrils are represented in many of the old Woodland designs. They are done with curved lines, and the overlay stitch is best suited for shaping them.

If you plan to decorate the instep piece of the moccasin, this must be done *before* the two sections are sewed together.

Draw up a full-size design of the beadwork on paper; then trace it onto the instep piece. See J. Start beading the large, central flower at its outer edge, as in K. Use a double thread and a bead needle, and string on 20 to 30 beads. When they are strung, insert the bead needle into the material near the design. Then place the row of beads along the edge of the design and, using another needle and thread, cast over the bead thread between every 6 beads. This is shown in L. When you reach the last 6 beads, string more beads on the first thread, if they are needed.

After the outlines are covered, fill in the centers, row after row, in the same way. See the inner lines

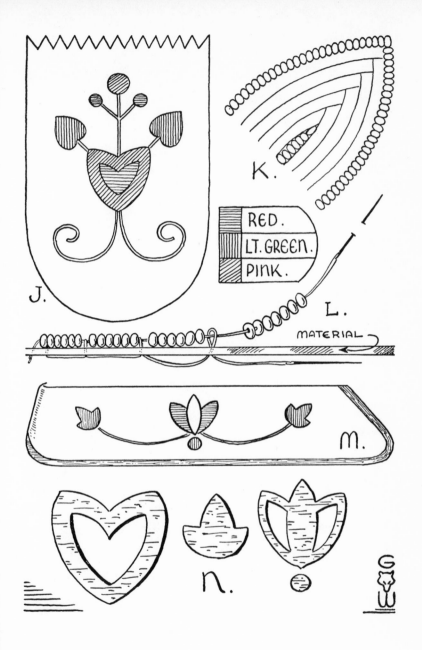

J.

K.

RED.
LT. GREEN.
PINK.

L.

MATERIAL

M.

n.

of K. Then cover the lower tendrils; these consist of only one row of beads each.

A matching design to be beaded onto the cuffs is given in M. Here the cuff has a narrow binding of cloth or tape. Such cuffs were sometimes covered with black or dark blue velvet, bound with tape, and then beaded.

In Woodland beadwork the same leaf or flower is sometimes repeated. To get the same effect each time, the Indians cut out a pattern of the design from birch bark. Cardboard will work just as well. See N.

13

Beaded Rosettes

BEADED rosettes were often used by the Indians to decorate war bonnets, knife sheaths, blanket strips, and neck ornaments. Large rosettes were made into belt bags. For modern use, rosettes can still serve many purposes. Among other things, they can be made into attractive pins, earrings, and necklaces.

The same stitch used to bead the Woodland knife sheath is used for beading rosettes. See A. As explained before, sew down 6 beads along the

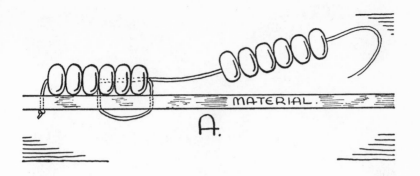

A.

outline of the design, and then return the needle and thread back to the top by drawing them through the center of the line of beads just sewed down. Then draw the needle and thread out through the last 3 beads, and string on 6 more.

In beading rosettes, start at the center and work out, as in B. The rows of beads are not spiraled; each circle is complete in itself.

Drawing C. shows a star design. Usually this design has a background of white beads, with the two vertical points of the star worked out in one color, the two horizontal points in another. No color suggestions are given here, but you might find it interesting to make a rosette pin in your school colors.

111

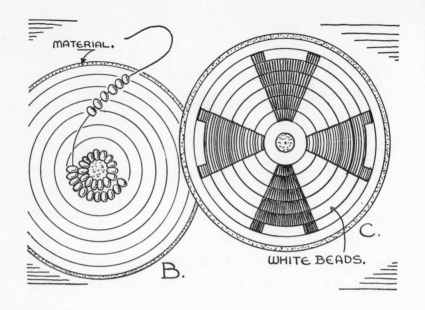

MATERIAL.

WHITE BEADS.

B.

C.

To make a rosette pin, draw a circle about 2 inches in diameter upon a piece of leather or felt. Trace the design onto the material and start the beading, changing from color to color as the design requires. When the beading is finished, cut a duplicate circle and sew a small safety pin to it, as in D. This should be sewed slightly above the center of the circle, so that the rosette will hang properly. Now sew together the beaded rosette and the backing. See E.

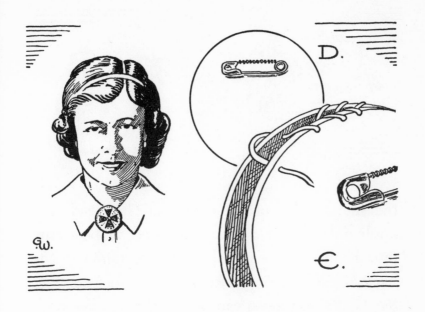

A bead edging, as described in Chapter 6, may be added to the rosette pin; or you can decorate it with a looped edging. To make this edging, string a few beads on a thread and sew each end of the beaded strand to the edge of the rosette so that it forms a scallop. Repeat this all around the edge of the rosette. See F.

To make a pair of matching earrings, cut out two circles about half the size of the pin and upon them draw a duplicate of the design, scaled to

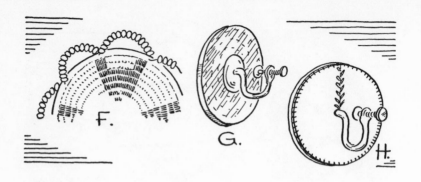

F.

G.

H.

the smaller size of the earrings. The beads are applied by the same method used to bead the pin. Then a screw attachment is fastened to the back of each earring with a little rubber cement. See G. These screws can be bought in a five-and-ten-cent store or at your local jeweler, or you can take them from a pair of old earrings. When you have cemented the screw to the beaded circle, cut out another circle for the back. Make a small slit in this piece from the edge to the center, so that it will fit over the screw. After the back is sewed to the front, this slit is sewed up, as in H. A bead edging, such as the one described in Chapter 6, can be added to the earrings to cover the sewing.

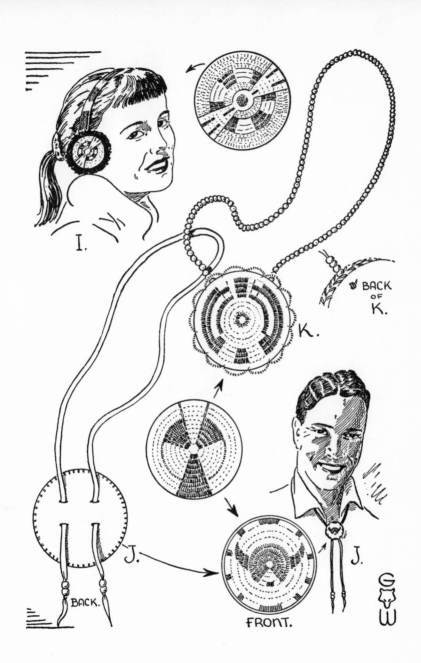

I.

K.

BACK OF K.

J.

BACK.

FRONT.

J.

For the winter, two rosettes of the proper size can be beaded and sewed to your ear muffs. See I.

Boys can use rosettes to make western bolo slides (tie slides), as shown in J. Here two pairs of small slits are cut into the backing before it is sewed to the rosette. A flat leather thong is inserted through the two left slits, looped under your shirt collar, and passed out through the two right slits. A pair of large beads is attached near each tip. Now slide the rosette up to the collar, so that the ends of the thong will hang below the rosette.

A rosette can also be made into a nice necklace by adding a string of pony beads, as in K. To do this, sew a double thread near the left edge of the rosette backing and string on beads until the strand is long enough to fit over your head. Then fasten the end of the thread near the right edge of the backing.

14
Bead Designs

AFTER you have tried your hand at beadwork, you may wish to continue and to venture farther afield.

First of all, you should know how to draw a diagram of a design. As mentioned in Chapter 2, one square inch of loom work requires 18 beads across the loom strings and 12 beads along the loom strings. Since the beads are slightly oval, they are longer than they are wide. Going along

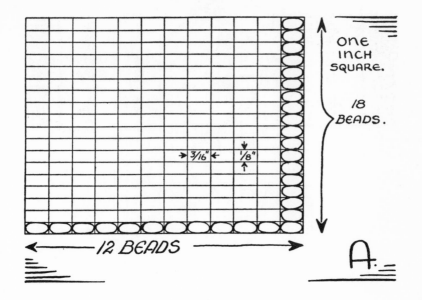

ONE INCH SQUARE.

18 BEADS.

3/16" 1/8"

12 BEADS

A.

the loom strings, the beads are placed end to end; going across the loom strings they are placed side by side. This means that it takes more beads to make one inch across the loom strings than it does to make one inch along the loom strings. For the same reason, the space between the horizontal lines should be about two thirds the size of the space between the vertical lines. Mark off this number of spaces on a piece of paper, but scale

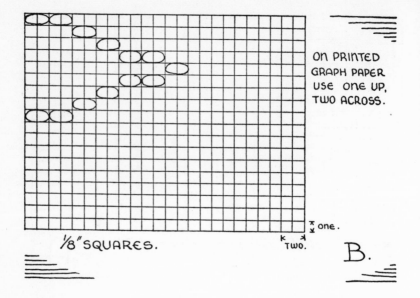

ON PRINTED GRAPH PAPER USE ONE UP, TWO ACROSS.

⅛" SQUARES.

one.

two.

B.

it to a larger size, as in A., so that it will be easier to work on. Now fill in the design, using one bead to each space.

Graph paper can also be used to make a diagram. But note that the length of one space in A. equals the length of two spaces on the graph paper, although the width remains constant. So plan your design accordingly. See B.

Designs can be enlarged by substituting a fixed number of added beads for every single bead in

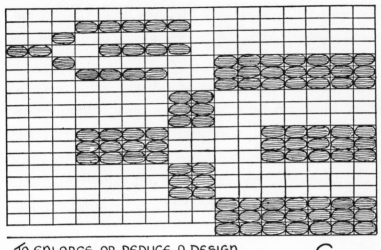

TO ENLARGE OR REDUCE A DESIGN.   C.

the original design. For example, 3 to 1 is the proportion used in the enlargement shown in C. By reversing the procedure, you can reduce a large design.

There are various sources for additional designs. You can use the drawings at the beginning of each chapter in this book. The design on the book jacket can also be copied. Local museums may have an Indian collection; if you ask their permission, they will probably allow you to copy the designs you desire. Pictures of Indians, especially large photographs, are also a source for designs.

The following pages of designs are drawn so that they can be made either on the loom or by using one of the stitching methods described in this book. By dividing the loom designs in strips 8 beads wide, you can work out these designs in the lazy stitch or in any of the other stitches mentioned.

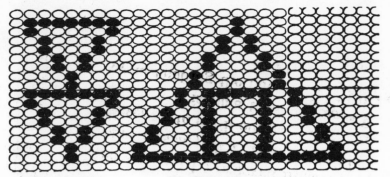

ARROW POINTS.   TEPEE OR TI - PI.

VERTEBRAE.   FEATHER.   MOUNTAIN.

CLOUDS.   ARROW.   HOURGLASS.

DRAGONFLY.   TREE.   LIGHTNING.   STAR.

FROM THE BASIC DESIGNS ON THIS PAGE MANY GOOD
COMBINATIONS CAN BE DRAWN FOR PATTERNS

G.W

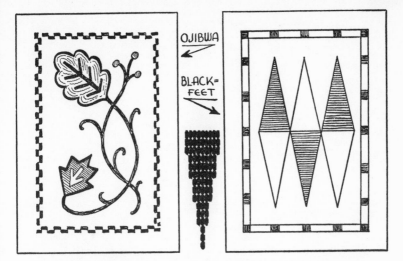

OJIBWA

BLACK=
FEET

ADDITIONAL BOOK-COVER DESIGNS

TOP DESIGN.

IROQUOIS HEADDRESS DESIGN ADAPTED TO BERET DECORATION.

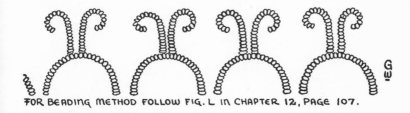

FOR BEADING METHOD FOLLOW FIG. L IN CHAPTER 12, PAGE 107.